AMPLIFY THOUGHTS

Author

Suzanne Massee

© Suzanne Massee 2018

Suzanne Massee is

the author of

Clarity

Thoughts Create

Conversations with Consciousness

Back to Basics

Back to Basics Harvest

Suzanne's Easy to Follow Baking Recipe's

Contents

Introduction	9
Appreciation	12
Activation	13
Addictions	14
Affirmations and Meditation	15
Alignment	16
All Eyes	17
Amplify	18
Appreciation and Gratitude	19
Appreciate All Things	20
Attention to a Subject	21
Attraction	22
Belief	23
Being More	24
Clarify	25
Clean Up	26
Clarity	27
Clarity of Thought	28
Contradictory Thoughts	29
Conditions	30
Continuation of Thoughts	31
Confidence	32
Control Your Vibration	33
Creation	34
Creating Problems	35
Creating is Thinking	36
Create your Experience	37

Creating Momentum 38
Creating 39
Define Deliberately 40
Deliberate Creator 41
Define Words 43
DE-Activate Old Thoughts 44
Desire for Better 45
Dis-Easement 46
Discipline is Focus 47
Discover New Thought 48
Dominate Intent 49
Dreams 50
Education and Imagination 51
Emotional Guidance 52
Emergence and Re-Emergence 53
Enlightenment is Alignment 54
Eternalness 55
Events into Reality 56
Every Thought Exists 57
Expand this Thought 59
Everything is NOW 60
Feeling Better 61
Feeling Place of Emotions 62
Fine Tuning 63
Feeling Place of Emotions 64
Fears 65
Feel Right Now 66
Fixation 67

Flow of Energy 68
Focus 69
Frequency of Energy 70
Gathering Vibration 71
Happy Emotion 72
Hatching Desires 73
Harmonizing Words 74
Harmonizing Path of Thinking 75
Influence to and Subject 76
Impulses 77
Ideas and Imagination 78
Imaginative Dreams 79
Intuitively 80
Indicators 81
Inner-Being is God 82
Infinite Intelligence Formula 83
Inner Guidance System 84
Illness and Influence 85
Indicators are Reflected 86
Inspiration 87
Inspiration is Revealed 88
Influence of Habit 89
Imagination is the Dream 90
In the Moment 91
In Between Times 92
Justify 93
Knowing 94
Key to Success 95

Law of Attraction is the Current 96
Love 97
Looking for Love in ALL the Wrong Places 98
Light Up 99
Liken to itself is Drawn 100
Leading Edge of Thought 101
Moods 102
Manifesting Process 103
Momentum of Thought 104
Magnified Thoughts 105
Mirroring 106
Man's Concept 107
Manifestation 108
Moulding Thoughts 109
Negative and Positive 110
Negative Emotion 111
Negative Feeling Emotion 112
Nobody is the Same 113
Nothing is a Lesson 114
No Doubt 115
No Absence 116
Observation 117
Origin of Thoughts 118
Observing 119
Observing Conditions 120
Power 121
Powerful Interaction 122
Problem or Solution Oriented 123

Pointing to Your Attraction	124
Pervasive Thought	125
Pervasive Thoughts	126
Powerful Flow	127
Perpetuation	128
Regret	129
Repetition	130
Repetition and Focus	131
Relationships	132
Relationships which are discorded	134
Relationship Attraction	135
Resistance	136
Resistance holds you back	137
Range of Emotions	138
Stimulator of Thought	139
Seeking Love	140
Solutions	141
Source Energy	142
Supplication Meaning	143
Separation from who you are	144
Spirit verses Human	145
Success	146
The Spiritual Self	147
The God force resides within	148
Timing and Alignment	149
Thinking Mechanisms	151
Thoughts	152
The Secret	153

Thoughts that Inspire 154
Think Better Thoughts 155
Think Feel and Focus 156
Thought is the Life Stream 157
Think and Feel 158
Transmitter and Transponder 159
The Law of Attraction 160
Watching you 161
Worthiness 162
What is itis 163
What Vibration are you on 164
Worry 165
Wanted or Unwanted 166
What's Bothering You 167
You are God 168
You Are Source Energy 169
You are the Attractor 171
You are Not Separate 172
The Author 173
More Inspiring Books by the Author 175
Social media 181

Introduction

Wouldn't it be nice to discover this powerful alignment which is within your eternal being, this eternal being is of well-being – it is alignment – it is happy – it is giving you the feeling indicators to your thoughts – it is of pure love – it is expanding with those positive thoughts – it does not flow with the negative thoughts which is why you feel such negative thoughts, it is your indicator telling you, that you are going the wrong way with those thoughts. This is powerful guidance and it can be felt, all you have to do is feel how you feel in the thoughts and once you do, you will be the realiser and the expander into new manifestations, and boundless expansion of becoming more, and the way to all of this expansion is to live and feel happy no matter what is going on around you, if you do not like what is going on around you, it is to focus your thoughts to topics that feel really good to you and to feel this happy feeling place, it is for you to find the magic within, and then the magic will become. Focus upon your thoughts and see where these thoughts arise from, is the thoughts coming from what you are observing or of a new thought that you know you could not have thought that thought, this is the inspirational thought to follow that thought.

The way to build momentum is to focus your thoughts, and to build up new thoughts, to read inspirational quotes, to watch a positive movie, to do what you like to do that makes you feel good, that makes you feel happy, and to feel the energy flow, find this flow, and your energy will rise.

Think about a time when something happened and you knew it was about to happen and you felt it so powerfully within, feel this magical time and re-live it, and feel that feeling again, this is you aligning, and letting your Inner-Being know how appreciative you were of this magical time, and then your Inner-Being will bring about more magical times.

Here are a few of my magical anecdotes;

I respond to nature in a powerful way and know the signs, I had a strong asking for my readiness, a sign to be for a bird to hit my window, of which has never happened, sounds cruel to the bird, but it was an asking way out of the ball park. The next day, while critiquing my book, two birds flew into my window landed on the ledge and chirped and sang and chirped and sang.

Once again, sometime later I asked again for a bird to come to my window for an answer to a question, and within seconds a bird flew to the fly screen and landed on it right in front of me, with strong asking and believing answers are delivered.

I became more focused and I had a strong asking for a punctuation to my alignment, while biking to the swimming pool my thoughts were I would like a punctuation and I looked up to the sky and saw a hawk, a hawk would definitely be a punctuation, the next day while at my computer I heard a commotion and looked up to see a hawk fly under the veranda and straight into my window.

On Christmas day while driving, I asked infinite intelligence 'When is the money going to rain on me' promptly a ten dollar note flew over my windscreen while I was driving; I certainly received what I asked for. Be aware of the choice of words used. What happens is the human population treats it as coincidences, they are not coincidences, they were on the way to you, and they were all in the asking for, by you. Then they promptly forget about the feeling or how they interacted to the thought that created the manifestation.

Now this is beautiful created manifestations to the thought flow, these thought flows also manifest the other side of the spectrum of dis-easement, accidents and negative interactions, it is all about your thoughts and where your thoughts are pointing too. Test the universe and be the realizer to your own thoughts, only you will know where your thoughts are taking you too.

Appreciation

My deepest appreciation that created and took my expansion to new heights was the teachings by Abraham

Infinite intelligence in the non-physical working through Esther Hicks in the physical.

Nothing is more pleasing than to listen to Abraham and to tune into an even higher vibrational energy.

It is the supreme art of the teacher to awaken joy in creative expression and knowledge: Albert Einstein

Activation

Everything is an activation of thought

If you see hate this is an activation and

the more you will see

If you see love this is an activation of more love you will see

If you see success this is an activation of more

Success you will see

If you see wellness this is an activation of more

Wellness you will see

If you see happy joyful this is an activation of more

Happy and joy you will see

If you see worthlessness this is an activation the more worthlessness you will see

It is all to do with the activation of the thoughts and in what you think and what you observe

This sounds so easy

Only people make it seem so difficult

Addictions

An addiction is a desire

To want to feel better

Drinking and drug taking in excess is an emotional imbalance and discord in your vibration. An addiction is a desire to want to feel better. These addictions are short term feel betters and cannot be maintained. Addictions within your body create your body cells to acclimate in your body and it will find a way to adapt and will want more to this adjustment and will adapt and want more, it is the momentum process. Any addiction can subside in a process by cleaning up your thoughts and cleaning up the memory cells within the body this can take just a few days. It is trusting the process and thinking it differently.

Affirmations and Meditation

Affirmations and Meditation

Promotes a faster vibration to your Inner Being

Meditation quiets the mind and allows the thoughts to become quiet gentle thoughts, it is to go into meditation with no resistance of what is wanted or not wanted of fixated desires, but a nothing thought to allow the thoughts to be communicated to you through your Inner Being.

Affirmations are a powerful energy building frequency by talking about yourself and how good you feel, how powerful you feel, it is using powerful statements about how you feel about you, increases a feeling within you this is your Inner Being agreeing with your affirmations, when you reach for the feeling and it feels really good you are tuned in, when you reach for thoughts that do not feel good or feel like hard work you will feel it, and this is the wrong way your Inner Being does not join you with this thought.

Alignment

Alignment is the work of the mind

It is in the thoughts

It is in the feelings

It is in the emotions you feel

It is in the reaching for good thoughts

It is making peace with where you are

It is letting go of resistant thoughts

The timing is all about alignment

How aligned and in fullness you are with you

All Eyes

All eyes (meaning non-physical)

is looking through the eyes of your Inner Being

These eyes only see purity

Only see good in all,

No matter what they are doing or whatever the conditions

These eyes appreciate implicitly

When you are connected to your Inner Being

Life feels joyful

Life is good and the more good you feel

The more good will come

Amplify

Amplify and gravitate

In or too

The same conditions with people

You then attract and amplify the way you are feeling

This is either in the feeling good or

The not feeling good momentum

Everything is attraction and it is the universal law

Appreciation and Gratitude

Appreciation is an expanding highly esteemed Enjoyment feeling word

It is a thought building word

It is an increase in value word

It is a momentum building word

Gratitude has a feeling of being grateful

Being grateful where you stand

It has a feeling of overcoming

It does not have the quality of a thought building word of appreciation which is an expanding word

We are all here for expansion in feelings, emotions and thought

To appreciate builds a momentum of emotion of appreciation feelings within

The feelings of all the emotions you feel

Is expansion

Is the key to all your wants and desires

Appreciate All Things

Appreciating all things

In all you are doing

In looking at conditions in appreciation

Pick out the best parts

Build upon the best parts brings about alignment

Attention to a Subject

The attention to a subject begins the subject

Choose the subject you want

Then focus and line up with the subject

If the subject does not feel good and does not give you the exciting feeling within

Then the subject is not the subject

Choose another subject

In time the feeling of elation will ripple through the body

Then line up with it

Work with it

Enjoy it

Imagine it

Dream it

Until the subject is dominate

Attraction

It is what you are giving emotional

Thought and feelings too

It is what you are creating into your vibration

It is your point of attraction and

What you are holding onto

Which will bring about the process

Of that momentum attraction vibration

Belief

A belief is only a thought you keep thinking

If it feels good, then you are in alignment with your

Inner Being your Higher Self

If you feel angst or off-ness of not feeling good

It is you separating you from your Inner Being

Your Inner Being is not following you

On this belief thought

The way you know

Is in how you feel

Being More

Words create the emotion

Words which are used are very powerful

Such as everything is already created

Everything is **IN** becoming

Not **TO** become, to say **TO**

Becomes in time, to come about

It is **IN** being **MORE**, not **TO** being more

Everything is now

Not later, but now

Feeling it now, not later

It is bringing the alignment of time into the now

This is all felt by the emotions you feel

Clarify

I want to **CLARIFY**

Something that is the basis of which

EVERYONE has

It is the awareness **EMOTIONS**

Emotion is a feeling

Feeling is an emotional vibration

It all starts from

A THOUGHT

Clean Up

How do you clean up old thoughts

By looking at the thought

Then look to another thought

Clarity

Clarity is lining up with something that is really clear

I like it

It makes me feel good

Clarity is in the transformation of the contrast

Into better feeling thoughts

Not to avoid the negative thoughts

But to transform and emphasis new better thoughts

Which makes me feel good

Clarity of Thought

Clarity becomes the indicator

Of the contrast of which you are

Feeling with those thoughts

Every thought has a contrasting thought

It is deciphering the contrasting thought

To what thought continuation you want to hold and maintain

The Source your Inner Being greatly enhances well-being and expansion of thoughts and desires through the process of pure thought, appreciative thoughts, appreciation into the feelings of the thought, and the appreciation of the appreciation, through the intentions of that thought, through the intentions of the feelings and the emotions, through unconditional appreciation, through unconditional love, through joy, through the words that create harmony and create up lift meant, through creating an atmosphere of the story, your desired story into a vibrational imagination of thought, and bringing this story into fruition, through appreciation regardless of the conditions of the present now. It is <u>You</u> being in the fullness with <u>You</u> in the present Now, in all that you do whether it be viewing, eating, speaking, relaxing, thinking, or observing, this is you rendezvousing with your Inner Being.

Contradictory Thoughts

Negative thought is a contradictory thought

Your Inner Being

The Source within does not see it that way

Which is why you feel the off-ness of that thought

The contrast of the thought evokes the decision

To feel a better feeling thought

Conditions

Love and appreciate the conditions in your present now

All conditions are clarifying you to who you want to become

These conditions are creating the momentum

To what universal law you are attracting

Continuation of Thoughts

The continuations of thoughts attract what you want

This is the Law of thought attraction

How easy can this be, I have to be aware of my very own thoughts; that is the key, and that is the Holy Grail to your Inner Being and to the collective life stream of this vibrational energy, which flows vibrational energies through you and receives vibrational energies from you.

Consider the thoughts that flow in and out throughout the day, what thoughts are you gathering momentum upon, are they pure positive thoughts or have you tipped the scale to negative thoughts, thoughts are the mood patterns that dictate the day, these emotional moods dictate to who you are in this moment, they dictate and expand to outside physical human forms, they can gather momentum and create havoc, this would not occur on a high vibrating vibration. Thoughts are powerful, thoughts are vibration, thoughts are transmittable and receivable; only give out thoughts that you want to vibrate with and what you want to be the receiver of.

Confidence

As you allow the focusing of thoughts to build

You gather the emotions to the feelings

You can begin to focus on more specific intention words

Upon what you want

When you speak in words or in your thoughts speak to the universe or your Inner Being as if you are at an interview and why you are the best person for the job, this is focusing the whole of you in building the momentum of the deliciousness of the job, momentum words; You have made the best decision – you have the confidence in me – I appreciate the confidence you have in me – I appreciate you have the confidence in my thoughts – the confidence in my words – the confidence in my emotions – the confidence in my communication – the confidence in me expressing and leading by my example – I appreciate the expansion in my confidence with who we are, and who I am, and it is exciting to deliberately create the environment to co-create, we will draw more like minded persons, this excites me, I love being the facilitator and conduit of Source, it is me – I appreciate the confidence you have in me it is exciting we can be, and do who and what we want to become – most of all I appreciate my Inner Being and the universal understanding of expansion.

This is the focusing of thoughts that it is already done and you are at the interview, and how exciting it is at this interview, just talk to in your thoughts to your most powerful tool which is your Inner Being. It is believing it before you see the evidence.

Control Your Vibration

You cannot control your surroundings

Or what is in the world

But you can control your vibration

Obstacles cross your path to realign and expand the whole of you to a greater expansion, this is a joyous occasion, and it allows you to look at what vibration you have activated, and defining what the contrast was meant to be, any contrast is redefining who you are, and bringing you further clarity to what momentum you are attracting.

You cannot control your surroundings or what is in the world, but you can control your vibration, your feelings and emotions to feel good, to feel your worthiness, to feel your thoughts, and your own alignment between you and you.

Creation

Desire is the beginning

Of all new Creation

Creating Problems

Holding or creating a problem is wasted energy

When solutions are so easy

When you observe a problem the problem is perpetuated and becomes magnified, it is only to look to a solution makes the adjustment to the vibration, most everyone's perspective is focused on many topics with such negativity, they talk about it, they media rise it, media thrives on negative momentum they believe this sells news, they have no idea that this form of media enhancement creates more of it, and then it is repeated, did I say repeated over and over again, if they were to see a new way and only place into media funny anecdotes, good feeling stories, winning stories, will bring about the good feeling emotion within all, this is creation, creation is creating, identify what you want to create. You have that choice of what you want to create and to what feel's good.

Creating is Thinking

Creating is thinking in thought

Of what you want and

How you want it to be

Create your Experience

You create your experiences

How you want to define those experiences

It is you who is allowing those experiences to flow more

Or to come to the clarity and release those unwanted thoughts

The mirroring effect is clarifying

You observe, you identify what you don't want

Then focus upon what you do want

Work on your imagination into focusing upon what you really do want

Creating Momentum

A person watching the news is verbally being vindictive to topics and creating and formulating his/her thoughts to the others when the others have not the same thoughts to the news, and expecting the others to follow in his/her thought belief, if verbal appraisal of the news is the creating momentum within the others it will become a momentum in this thought process and this is how actions of others create a movement of flow, it is choosing what you want to talk about, hear about, and speak about.

Creating

Every single person has come here to create

But not in the way you think your brain is creating

But creating from the vantage point from

Your Inner Being guiding and encouraging you

To the intentions that you have placed into

A vibrational escrow over many life times

If it were conceivable of who we are and this unseen frequency vibrational energy which is disregarded because it is unseen, if it were true and that you can tap into this resourceful universal Collective Consciousness, and if possible we tuned into this frequency, and allowed this communication to interact with us, and this communication is spoken to you by form of emotion to what is next, then wouldn't it be nicer to live and be and do who we want to be, and this is the very essence of what you came here to do, instead of just co-existing and not creating.

Define Deliberately

The moment you begin to care about how you feel

Is the moment you begin

To define your journey deliberately

You will begin to ride the wave instead of

Tumbling in the cog mire of the breakers

Deliberate Creator

A conscious deliberate creator is aware of the emotions, is aware of the responses, is aware of the choices, is willing to feel good with the responses within the emotions to the choices and is aware of the responses which equal the conscious alignment between you and you. You become the deliberate feeler; you feel into your imagination your desires and your dreams.

A deliberate creator chooses the alignment and deliberately brings into existence through emotions and imagination the desired path or alignment to what is wanted, a deliberate creator knows and feels the existence of the universal forces and taps into this resourceful energy to create and become more. The deliberate creator clarifies the emotions and knows what is being observed of what is, is what you will get, more of what is wanted or unwanted.

Whereas creating by default is not aware of the choices, and not aware of what the emotions is telling them, is not aware of the responses to the choices. Law of attraction then responds to the responses of those choices that are made automatically without active consideration and or viable alternative choices and options to decisions.

The default effect is the absence of the willingness of feeling a viable alternative; it is a pre-set choice that will be used if no choice is created, it becomes action oriented and most of the times these decisions do not play out to your advantage. When you come to feel the emotions within, you will feel the off-ness to the decision taken.

Whereas the deliberate creator is willing to feel good, is willing to feel the emotional responses to the feelings of the choices.

Define Words

Define feeling words and what it feels and means to you, these words are triggers to you; they begin a feeling behaviour and a focusing point to focus on the feeling. The feeling is the first manifestation; the details will fill in once you have established the feelings of the thought.

For example, the word Abundance feels like fullness, feels like ease, value, confidence and flow. Massage the word until you feel a feeling within. Words used will evoke a feeling, and when you discover this feeling place within you this is when you can play with more words.

Write or think each of these words and feel how you felt with each word, focus on the feeling, it is the process of becoming more in the focusing of feelings, and this is where it is all at, this is where all that you want and to become starts. Allow the flow of each word and play with each word in your mind and words will just flow and escalate into further feeling emotional words.

DE-Activate Old Thoughts

DE- active old thoughts

Old thoughts are just old thoughts

They no longer serve you, and

Will hold you where you are

You are here to create new thoughts

Desire for Better

No matter where I am

There is a good reason for me to be here

No matter what

I am and they are not in a wrong place

You become to recognise these emotional feelings

It becomes a clarifying moment

A desire for better

Trust in this power of energy

Dis-Easement

Perpetuation of any dis-easement

Is created in thought

The Source your Inner Being within, never joins you in your discomfort or dis-easement for the discomfort and dis-easement is not the Source with in's eternal path, it is you pointing in the opposite of who you really are, that is why you feel the discomfort and allow the dis-easement of thought patterns to take hold of you.

A dis-easement can run prevalent within families, this is creating it by talking about it, thinking about it, placing focus upon it, it is giving it more oxygen and the more oxygen you give it, the more it becomes, it is to refocus and not give it the air time, this is how you stop the momentum of any dis-easement. Focus upon harmonising thoughts;

I appreciate that my Inner Being is expanding me to my desires of well-being. I really love knowing that it is all about my focus.

I really love knowing I can begin my day in well-being, I love knowing that it is my focus that creates my day.

I really love knowing that I am able to discern my own vibration, I love the feeling, and it feels so wonderful.

I really love knowing that I can focus my thoughts. I love knowing that I can guide my thoughts and behaviour. I love knowing I can change my conditions by easing and realigning my thoughts.

Discipline is Focus

Be aware of negative emotion

Bless it

It is the indicator of change

To catch the emotion before it gathers momentum

Discipline is in your focus of thoughts

Discover New Thought

Through discovery you will imagine and realise that the imagination is the realiser of desires

Imagine to be the receiver of the imagined desires

Imagine it so often and train into the expectation of the imagined desires being realised, and how it would feel, this is tuning into your Inner Being and bringing the imagined thought into reality

This is powerful creating

Dominate Intent

Being non-resistant is to take the effort to shift your emotions

To shift your thoughts to the least resistant thoughts

One at a time, until you are in alignment

Your major dominate intent is to feel good, is to feel alive, is to feel wonderful, when you are fully engaged and are being truly who you are, this is the way you are supposed to feel and anything less than that you are off your path

Dreams

Dreams are the portal to your Source, they portray events, and they portray what you are feeling in your current point in time.

Dreams can inspire events or to take action on the event, dreams can be an instant manifestation or a prophesised event into the future to take place, or an inspired dream to believe in the event that will eventuate. It is for you to feel the quality of the dream and how you felt in the dream; these are the indicators of where your point of attraction is.

Dreams that have the nightmarish tones are portraying what is currently happening in your now and where your vibration is. These dreams can inspire better outcomes or better outcomes in thought and feelings and for better outcomes in where your point of attraction is here, in the now.

Education and Imagination

You bring the reality in, of which is in your imagination of what you want

In other words, reality does not exist

It is the thoughts that bring about the reality

Reality only exist it you keep on perpetuating it

Reality then becomes the wanted or unwanted desires

Imagination is the only key to success

Education is prevalent in holding onto past life experiences and keeping it alive, and so much energy is taken up with past tense historical experiences of which are not even relevant in the here and now. It appears to be the way for education to fill in a school curriculum instead of enhancing an imaginative experience. Education has become and is taking away from the very essence of who you and they are of which is imagination, discovering imagination, discovering inner motivation, discovering how to manifest desires and dreaming your desires, and expanding thought beyond thought, having fun and play. But instead we will teach about the lost lives of war, which just creates more wars, this is not expansion of any physical beings. If they only knew that to meditate, draw, sing and play brings about the flow of energy quicker and faster than slogging to death past life experiences. It is the interaction and bouncing of thought and how to feel in thought, and how to feel the emotions to the thought, this is the real education; this is where it is all at.

We are now looking forward not recreating past life experiences that is not moving forward.

Emotional Guidance

This is a vibrational universe, we are here to remember our own emotional guidance system, and we are here to tap into the indicators of this emotional guidance.

Once you get it

It takes discernment of your relationship of your emotions, feelings and thoughts, and to what vibrational atmosphere you are activating to these emotions

Emergence and Re-Emergence

To eat or not to eat meat

If you were to discover that this is a belief thought that has been perpetuated by those who have no understanding of this life stream of energy, the meat you are eating is not the spirit or the soul, that spiritual part of them remerged and then precede to re-emerge again and again, they appreciate the joy of providing themselves to be enjoyed because they know there is no death, it is the human part who thinks they know, and feels a belief in trauma, whereas the trauma is only within themselves, everything is thought if you think it you will believe it, and will follow with that belief, and bring others into that belief thought form, it all comes down to how do you really feel, and if you are having a traumatic issue and feeling it, it is not coming from the pure positive vibrational energy because your Inner Being does not feel it this way. Get to the feeling and feel how the emotions feel and then you make choices on your own discovery, and the discovery is that there is no death just emergence and re-emergence and the joy in the creation, of recreating. Doesn't the bible fore tell the rising of Jesus, it is already known the eternalness of oneself, and they are all still waiting for the rising, when he has emerged into so many other lives already.

Enlightenment is Alignment

True alignment comes forth from the universal non-physical stream of infinite intelligence energies, guiding the lit path; signs emerge into relation to what you desire, from your dominate thought pattern. When you allow in the vibration into receiving, then this vibration translates into thought, or vision, or hearing, or knowing.

Indicating signs are reflected all around you, by way of songs, if a song is being persistent in thought, look at the song, look at the lyrics, what is non-physical infinite intelligence trying to tell you or guiding you too. A song can play at the very moment you have a thought or question, being in true alignment you will recognise instantly the message relayed to you.

A thought may pop into your head that is a thought completely out of the blue, look at it and observe the message infinite intelligence non-physical is guiding you, 'this way-this way'.

When you are tuned into vibration occurrences start to be played out, you are placed at the right time, in the right place to open doors. Or processes are played out to evolve you onto a greater understanding of your expansion of your Source energy, and when aligned with the desires which you have created in imagination the non-physical brings about the manifestations of the desires.

Eternalness

The God force resides within

You and Me, as

You and Me

This God force is your Inner Being which is the older wiser part of you who has lived many life times, and now you are here as an extension of this older wiser part of you expanding your own energy stream for more expansion, to become more, and when you decide to depart the real world, your energy stream will become another physical being for the extension of your older wiser part of you, and this life stream will expand and become more, this creation is never ending.

Events into Reality

It is working with your Inner Being who works to bring the event into the reality, in saying this it is you that has to do the imagery work, your Inner Being is the keeper of the imagery, until there is so much emotional feeling to it, that it has to be realised by you to enjoy.

Every Thought Exists

You have this electrical charge of vibrational energy vibrating within you and it is created with thought then into an emotion and into a feeling.

If you consider that you are all thinking mechanisms of thinking, you are always thinking, you are always dreaming, you are always imagining where do you think these thoughts come from, there are many piles of thought waves, some of these piles are of momentous proportions of good feeling thoughts, and not so good feeling thoughts, some thoughts have a strong asking, and some thoughts hold a strong resistance, these thoughts collectively form and create more thought, with these thoughts it is to identify the emotion behind the thought and to which emotion you want to activate, a good feeling thought activates a positive flow of energy and a happy thought activates a response to the subjects of thoughts and is always finding the solution, a resistant thought or unhappy thoughts activates more of the same thoughts and stays in the problems. Pervasive belief of thought creates whatever you are asking for, and everything is an asking for, because if you keep the thought alive it just becomes more. The more you observe the more the thoughts create to what is being observed, it is in the focusing of what is been observed in a changed thought, and the thoughts you create can alter the behaviour of the observed thought. It is the mistrust or not knowing in how you feel in the physical human form which is an emotional response to a thought; this is not taught or even acknowledged that the happy emotion is the response to all happy solutions, an emotion that is resistant in thought can become the response to an illness, it is the pervasive thoughts that create the disconnection to your Inner Being.

Expand this Thought

Feel how you feel when you hatch a new thought desire feel how exciting this feels, this is a new thought that your Inner Being desires for you. But what most everyone does is disallows this thought to flow, and then doubts it, this is when you are not up to speed with this desire that you have hatched, it is for you to focus into more thoughts to that thought hatched desire. You have to expand this desire into your imagination, until you become so in tune and familiar with this desire.

Everything is NOW

Everything is **NOW**

When a thought pops in from days gone by

Change the thought to **NOW**

What you want **NOW**

Not yesterday's thought

All eyes (meaning non-physical) is looking through the eyes of your Inner Being, these eyes only see purity, only see good in all, no matter what they are doing or whatever the conditions, these eyes appreciate implicitly, when you are connected to your Inner Being, life feels joyful, life is good and the more good you feel, the more good will come.

Then you will come to a point where you will feel the energy of NOW, everything is NOW, when a thought pops in from days gone by, change the thought to NOW and what you want NOW, not yesterday's thought, that thought will keep you in that vibration and more so if it is a negative thought, slide the thoughts to the present and build upon what is wanted into emotional harmonizing thoughts, and why you want your desires to be manifested. Focus upon the goal post of what is wanted, and feel the present emotion of now, enjoy what is NOW, if you cannot focus on what is in the present conditions of NOW, focus your thoughts in the direction of what makes you happy, anything that keeps the uplifting feelings within.

Feeling Better

This emotional guidance vibration is so sophisticated, and yet so simple, it is the sophisticated mood guidance, the worse you feel the worse the feeling will replicate, and the better you feel the better the feeling will expand, and when you are in a place of alignment where conditions are occurring, and you can stand in a place of not reacting to the conditions but observing from a place of no resistance, this is achieving the art of alignment.

Feeling Place of Emotions

Consciousness your Inner Being your Higher Self, gives an emotion that is felt, if you are not feeling an emotion it is not consciousness, it is you putting out the thought, it is to become sensitive to the feeling place of emotion. It is to get to the emotional feelings first, understand the emotional feelings first, this is the first step. Get there first and all the rest will just happen.

Fine Tuning

Knowing is a powerful alignment

It begins the fine attunement of tuning your frequency

To that knowing of well-being

True alignment is that all knowing, how you know you just know, even though you cannot see it, or touch it, you just know, it then begins the progression of trusting, believing, and bringing yourself up to speed in tuning your vibration with the Source within, which then is reflected out into the universe, for the universe to reflect back to you.

Feeling Place of Emotions

It is getting to this feeling emotional place first

This is the true manifestation

When this is achieved first

All that you want will come to you

Fears

One who fears has it most in their vibration

Brings that feared subject into reality

Feel Right Now

The only thing that makes the difference in the way you feel right now

Is the **thought** that you are **thinking right now**

It doesn't matter how much money you've got; there are joyful people with no money, and there are unhappy people with lots of money. How you feel is about how you are allowing the Source that is You, to flow through You.

Fixation

Most live life for another and are fixated upon another for their happiness, when nothing is left but only you, all you have is you, so you is all there is, so if this is the case you have every right to be selfish and be you, and find you, then thoughts cannot be misplaced but observed into what is right for you, not for them, because you cannot live or think the thoughts for another.

Flow of Energy

You are all of the flow of energy

This energy flows through you

You are The Source

You are all Gods seeking the joyful vibration of truly being God in all its pureness and maintaining being the totality of being the willing representative, the willing participator of The Source.

We are all vibrating energy and receiving vibrational energy which is perceived in and by the non- physical part of you that resides within you, which you call your soul, or spirit, or spiritual self, or your inner being, and it is felt in the here and now in the physical reality of The Self. You can never detach or disconnect from this vibration, it exists forever, even in death, and re-emerges again. It is the energy life stream of your many life time experiences and it is forever building to an even greater expansion of you.

Focus

Focus and think happy thoughts

Find a reason to feel good when you wake up

Feel the frequency of love

Feel the frequency of enthusiasm

Feel the frequency of fun

Feel these frequencies without thinking about anyone or anything and allow the feeling to these frequencies to come through, identify how each of these frequencies feel within and then thoughts will follow through. These thoughts are created in the perfect moment of the flow, and the flow flowing through you, is the feeling of a powerful flow of thoughts.

Frequency of Energy

This is not a physiological trip; this is an emotional vibrational universe, and everything is a vibrating frequency of energy, and you feel this through your emotions.

Momentum of thought reverts to emotional feelings, these are indicators to what point of attraction that you are in vibration with, and if you have good feeling thoughts, positive joy and appreciation thoughts you are on the vibrational path that is becoming the true alignment of who you really are, and with your Inner Being your own Source.

If the momentum of thought is pointing you into a dark heavy energy, and your emotions are spiralling out of control, and you feel out of whack you are on a vibrational pattern that is not in true alignment to who you really are, or to become, the Inner Being within you knows when you are out of synch to who you are meant to be, these feelings are not from The Source, for The Source is of pure energy and is giving indicators to change your emotions, this is your mood indicator to where you are standing at every moment in time. Every time you feel your mood dive, always remember this is not The Source within, it is you that has deviated from your Inner Being your Source, The negative emotion you feel is you not taking the bounce to where your Inner Being is, it is you, still looking at what is, take the bounce - you have to keep up with you.

Gathering Vibration

Where does our imagination go and come about, You all have a vibrational escrow a filing system of all the wants you want to experience of which has been gathered over many life times it is there percolating and waiting for you to feel, and to come up to speed with it.

It is to feel how you feel when you think about the thing you want, if it feels good and the body ripples with goose bumps you have been acknowledge with your Inner Being and that this is a good thought and this is the vibration to work to, it is to believe in this feeling and find the way to the desired want, what slows the speed is ignoring the relayed feeling, and by the negative thoughts, and doubting.

Happy Emotion

A Happy emotion

Is the response to all

Happy solutions

It is the mistrust or not knowing in how you feel in the physical human form which is an emotional response to a thought; this is not taught or even acknowledged that the happy emotion is the response to all happy solutions, an emotion that is resistant in thought can become the response to an illness, it is the pervasive thoughts that create the disconnection to your Inner Being.

Hatching Desires

Feel how you feel when you hatch a new thought desire feel how exciting this feels, this is a new thought that your Inner Being desires for you. But what the physical human does is disallows this thought to flow, and then doubts it, this is when you are not up to speed with this desire that you have hatched, it is for you to focus into more thoughts to that thought hatched desire. You have to expand this desire into your imagination, until you become so in tune and familiar with this desire. It is then and only then that the universe, collective consciousness brings this desire into manifestation.

Harmonizing Words

I love the idea that I can create my own reality

No! I can say it better, I am creating my own reality

I like the idea that I am getting better and better at it

I like the idea of being focused in the here and now

I like the idea that this environment stimulates me to new ideas

I really like knowing this environment has a lot of choices

I am coming into clarity with new ideas with my focusing

I like this environment

No! I can say it better I really love this environment

Harmonizing Path of Thinking

Be aware in what you say and think

Think only of what you want

You will discover to look at life differently

You will discover a harmonising path of thinking, saying and doing it better, this path is the path to true alignment, stay on this path and you will be the receiver of all good things to come into your experience.

Influence to and Subject

The influence to any subject that being health and well-being, relationships, money, environmental occurrences around planet earth, all these occurrences brings about emotional manifestation which you feel, they become more, the more you put thought to it, or speak it, the more it is.

Take attention to what is naturally flowing to you, not what is observationally flowing around you.

Impulses

The impulse is felt and you will have this feeling emotional urge to just go and buy that lottery, to take that road, to ring that person, to read that article, these impulses is the Inner Being saying do it, and do it now not later but now, many of these impulses are lost in translation because the physical human form has not understood the feeling emotion to the impulses, and many opportunities are lost for an easier nicer path.

Ideas and Imagination

Ideas and imagination

What is the difference?

An idea is a thought to an idea for evolution, you take an idea and expand on the idea and when enough get onto the idea it becomes a Collective Consciousness thought form and the idea expands and will become more and when the idea is fully aligned it becomes a manifestation into the reality.

The process for the imagination is the physical human form creates an imagination in thought of what they really desire, and imagines in great detail how it would feel, and to acclimate to the desired outcome in such specific detail that it becomes a reality, to be enjoyed now.

Imaginative Dreams

We are all here to live our imaginative dreams

We are all here to bring the dreams into full manifestations.

If these dreams, we have were not within us

We would not have a way to our future

If we keep looking at where we are and behind us

We can't see what is ahead of us.

Intuitively

The moral of the story is to listen to that inner voice that keeps on giving you the thought, and act upon it, it just may surprise you.

Intuitively I kept on getting an inner thought all day "Get your passport" I had wanted to change my passport back to my maiden name, but I was not financially able too. Finally, I listened to this thought and applied for the papers to be sent. A few days later they arrived, and I did say to infinite intelligence "Are you happy now it is here" perusing through the fine print I was completely gobsmacked! it said if you have two years left on your passport and you have been divorced within the year the passport can be changed free of charge, I fitted all these categories. The moral of the story is to listen to that inner voice that keeps on giving you the thought, and act upon it, it just may surprise you.

Indicators

Source is of pure energy and is giving indicators to change your emotions; this is your mood indicator to where you are standing at every moment in time.

Every time you feel your mood dive, always remember this is not The Source within, it is you that has deviated from your Inner Being your Source

The negative emotion you feel is you not taking the bounce to where your Inner Being is

It is you, still looking at what is

Take the bounce - you have to keep up with you

Inner-Being is God

If we were to change the word God to Inner Being

We may see a better society

Because the God word just keeps everything separate

You can never be separate

For you are it

Infinite Intelligence Formula

Reality

Is living life in the physical. Observing Reality

Observe what you really want for you

Sift and sorting Reality. Sort out what it is and focus

Desire

The focus becomes a desire

Imagination

Imagination is the focusing tool

Thoughts

Thoughts are gathered to this focus

Emotion/Feelings

This becomes an emotion and feeling place to the focus desired thoughts

Joy and Satisfied with the thoughts

Joy and satisfaction is where vibration creates momentum of flow

Vibration

The emotion becomes a vibration and is felt by Infinite Intelligence, and if it is of joy and satisfied with the thought and the intent of the thought it becomes a manifested reality.

Manifestation

The manifestation becomes a reality, by applying and having consistency to the laws of the universe and living and adapting to these principles.

Inner Guidance System

Teach your children this inner guidance system

Teach them to understand and feel emotions

To identify emotions and feelings

Teach children to feel emotions, is what you as parents are here to create in them as well as yourselves, you are not here to create their direction they have their own inner guidance system helping and guiding them to who they want to become and do. Teach your children this inner guidance system; teach them to understand and feel emotions, and to identify emotions and feelings. To dream, to dream big, to quiet the mind, the still mind brings about thought, this is where all the answers are and arise from, imagine all possibilities, to love themselves, if they feel unloving, create a feeling in them with positive words, you are an ingenious creator, you are beautiful, you are so loving, you are clever, I love how you do this, I am proud of you, I imagine love and joy for you, I can feel your loving. Create an atmosphere to love themselves even in their unwillingness to love, for this will truly open the heart and love and alignment is where it all happens, this is above all physical manifestations, this is the realiser to fulfil and manifest desires, and most of all to trust in their own guidance system and to be happy. Being happy and having fun is where it is all at, this is the vibration where it all happens.

Illness and Influence

Attention to an illness influences the illness

Onto another or onto the unborn child

If they are taking on that thought which begins to be an emotion

This emotion to the illness becomes more and becomes a

Vibration and an illness into their experience

It is as simple as an illness, the parents talk about someone in the family having it, you create it as an incurable illness, and call it hereditary, you keep the illness alive, it is the thought which creates the thought to the illness, if you were to change the thought and leave it in the delete pile, it is then deleted, but you as humans cannot seem to do this, you hear someone else talk about the illness and then the old thought re-emerges again, and becomes active in your thoughts again, this is what creates the illness, if you were to delete and give it no oxygen the illness would become non-existent and an irrelevant topic.

The generations of families keep on perpetuating what they had onto their children, they have nothing better to say but with what they had, and then the innocents of the children take on their thought belief.

Then you are bomb blasted and driven with the illness by media, by charity marches, by funded projects, this just keeps on perpetuating the process, it takes a very powerful human to override this thought and belief process, and when you get it, you will be set free from this incurable illness.

Indicators are Reflected

True alignment comes forth from

The universal non-physical stream of infinite intelligence energies, guiding the lit path

Signs emerge into relation to what you desire

From your dominate thought pattern

How are indicators reflected; the laws of the universe is a vast pulsating vibrational energy of infinite intelligence, it feels, it feels emotions, it feels thoughts, when meaningful emotions are reflected, and it becomes the true essence of who you want to become, the universe works alongside you guiding you, giving you the indicators, are you open to view, feel or hear these indicators;

Inspiration

Inspiration comes through with which

Emotional vibration you are on

Inspiration comes through with which emotional vibration you are on, if you are in anger the anger perpetuates and may be inspired to take an action that is discorded to who you really are, if you are in depression the depression perpetuates by your inspired thoughts of depression, inspiration is perpetuated in many forms of what thought you are courting, it is reaching for thoughts of fun, happiness and enjoying what is now is where the wholeness of you is, this is where your outcomes and desires is peculating, and will be released to you. Test the universe you may be very surprised how this energy stream works.

Inspiration is Revealed

Inspiration is right there

It is always being revealed; you will realise it by not blocking it.

Allow the feeling emotion in, not making it happen

But feel and find the precision in the feeling manifestation

By becoming the realiser of the emotional vibration of the laws of the Universe process, and leaving out the habit of thought by releasing resistance brings about the inspired action, this is the feeling to take that road, to go and buy the lottery, it is listening to this inner voice that keeps popping up, or this deep feeling do something without knowing why to do this. To allow the manifestation of all the desires that have been formulating in vibration to full blown manifestation, is allowing the indicators to the inspired action to take you to the place of action, without you creating the action of what you are wanting but to allow the action to be inspired within you, this is the whole of you coming together with your Inner Being to the full realisation of who you are and to who you want to be in this life time experience. You want to be inspired into action, and not dictate the action. The inspired action is the resistance to the habit of thought this allows infinite intelligence to bring about the inspired event. An inspired event is the resistance of habit of thought.

Influence of Habit

Most everyone keeps on perpetuating what is

By the influence of habit

by your invitation of the influence of habit

You added this influence onto you

Most everyone have an unhappy life and expect the same for others, and then they talk about it, they gather groups about it, they publicise it, this reasoning just keeps on expanding and creating it into more and more, like minded humans gather it then has this has a rolling effect, and then they say it is true we all have it, without them even realising that the more you talk about it the more it becomes, this is the thought process that most everyone does not understand, it is the thoughts they create is who they are becoming, and if they stopped the thoughts becoming they will release the condition's.

Imagination is the Dream

You were all given thoughts

All know what the imagination can do and bring about

The imagination is the dream

The dream came from the imagination

If conceivable where the thoughts arise from, and how the imagination builds the thoughts, and then to consider is it your thoughts, or are you tuning into this unseen Inner Being your Higher Self, the larger broader part of you.

You would tap into this resourceful universal power and have no doubts about its ability to deliver. It is to ask and through a process of believing, the asking is given.

In the Moment

Feeling good is always in the now

It is what you are doing right now

Right this second

It is how you are feeling

It is the whole of you present in the moment of the now

Not later not yesterday

But what is right now

It is being in the fullness of you in whatever you are doing

In Between Times

It is what you do in the in between times

How happy are you

Are you treating each moment as fun or a new experience?

Are you appreciating?

Are you feeling in the flow?

This is the important relevant step to all processes

You cannot have a happy ending from an unhappy place

Justify

Well-meaning people who are conducive in holding people where they don't want to be, and it is to justify where they are, you have your own power and ability to make your own decisions.

Knowing

True alignment is that all knowing

How you know you just know, even though you cannot see it

Or touch it, you just know

It then begins the progression of trusting

Believing, and bringing yourself up to speed

In tuning your vibration with the Source within

This is then reflected out into the universe

For the universe to reflect back to you

Knowing is a powerful alignment

It begins the fine attunement of tuning your frequency

To that knowing of well-being

Key to Success

You are bringing the reality in

Of which is in your imagination of what you want

In other words, reality does not exist

It is the thoughts that bring about the reality

Reality only exist if you keep on perpetuating it

Reality then becomes the wanted or unwanted desires

Imagination is the only key to success

Law of Attraction is the Current

Law of attraction is a current

It is the current which you are flowing too

It is the current providing for you to decide which way to go

You will feel the flow of the current

If it feels good go with the flow

If it does not feel good don't do it

If it feels hesitation you are not ready for it yet

Let your imagination grow with the idea some more

You will feel when the time is right

Love

Find the love and appreciation of you

See the beauty in all others

Even in all their contrasting issues

They came into this life time experience with love and beauty

They are here to find their own path to it

You shine your light

Like a moth they will be drawn to this light

Looking for Love in ALL the Wrong Places

Almost everyone is looking for love in all the wrong places

They think if they have someone

They will feel better in the having of it

Most times they are not happier but more miserable Finding faults

The love to discover first and foremost is the love of oneself

Then the lover you want will become what you want

It is creating what you want first

Light Up

There are many ways to explain

In each explanation it will become a feeling within

It is to feel your way to it

It is to feel the emotion

It is not to think your way to it

The thinking is the process to find the feelings to the emotional words used

It is not to over think it

If it lights up as an emotional feeling

This is the response that

You are in unison with your Inner Being

Liken to itself is Drawn

That is liken to itself is drawn

Everything in the universe is magnifying and

Drawing unto oneself

The more you say I don't want that

The more you are giving the attention to what you do not want

The universe is only feeling and hearing what you do not want

It is to think the thoughts to what you do really want

Only focus on what you do really want

It is to feel the emotion within the focus

This is your Inner Being working in harmony with that focus

Leading Edge of Thought

Source views the world through you and expands through you.

You are a representative of this Source vibrational energy stream, a representative of deliberately creating and deliberately manifesting your creations, you are right here, right now at the leading edge of thought.

Thought and your emotions is the process how the universe interacts with you, and you must be on that vibration for the universe to deliver your desires into manifestations, and there is nothing more satisfying and more fulfilling and more exciting than to be a deliberate creator.

Moods

Identify the mood, the emotions that you are manifesting into your experience. The secret is in identifying your thoughts your mood and how you feel, and where those thoughts and feelings are taking you, is this the right momentum of feelings that you are creating within you, once you identify these thoughts and can bring about a better feeling, a better emotion to those thoughts this is when you are truly in alignment to who you are wanting to become.

Manifesting Process

The manifesting process is the emotion first; you feel the emotion

Then the thought

Thought and emotion work simultaneously

Notice the emotion then put emphasis on the thought that caused the emotion

Momentum of Thought

We all came forth eagerly to expand and achieve momentum of thought, and to decipher contrast and alignment, most of all to align and remember the older wiser part of you which has lived and experienced many eternal reality life paths, reaching for the fulfilment of pure wholeness and becoming more, and expanding more.

Magnified Thoughts

All thoughts are magnified and that is

Likened to itself is drawn

You will hear the parents say to the child 'that is just the way it is, get over it' that is the parents bondage and their own thought process the child has its own intentions, and the child knows better, but for the bondage of the parent it then is drawn into that thought process. The child will feel and become confused, and for most they begin to disconnect to the excitement they felt when they decided to live in a human form.

Mirroring

The concept of mirroring is a mirror of you

It is observing like upon like

That is likened to oneself is drawn

Situation upon situation

It is observing you in how you are feeling

Man's Concept

The Source views, the term being Vengeful, or a vengeful God.

This is exactly Godly in man's concept of God, which is formed through the image of man's mind, what man calls God speaks vengeance, man's concept of God is not the perspective of Infinite Intelligence of what God is.

This life stream of energised vibration is purity, and vengeance is not purity, vengeance is created by physical human forms completely out of alignment.

Manifestation

Manifestation is evidence of alignment

Whether with the wants or don't wants

You create your experiences; and how you want to define those experiences, and it is you who is allowing those experiences to flow more, or to come to the clarity and release those unwanted thoughts. The mirroring effect is clarifying, you observe, you identify what you don't want, and then focus upon what you do want, and work on your imagination into focusing upon what you really do want.

Moulding Thoughts

More is what you are

The more you are

The more you become

It is converting the thoughts to already having and

Wanting and having more

It is moulding the thoughts to that which you already have it

And expanding the thoughts to more

Negative and Positive

It is as simple as your thoughts

You have a choice, to change the thought pattern

We all have a yin and a yang

We all have a dark and a light side

A negative a positive, an opposite to a thought

It all depends on which one you are courting

It is the duality in wants and unwanted

It is what you give your attention to

"Whatsoever a man soweth

That shall he also reap" Galatians 6:7

Negative Emotion

Negative emotion is the most practised emotion

It feels normal to most everyone

It is to recognise this negative emotion

And clean it up

Negative Feeling Emotion

A negative feeling emotion is only the indicator that you have some resistance to clean up on that topic, because all topics should be looked at in the attitude of, all is okay and nothing is wrong here, because what you are making wrong is not how your Inner Being sees it, because you Inner Being sees it right and looking at the rightness while you are looking at the wrongness, and what you feel as wrongness is the right place for you to become a forward focuser and not a what is itis focuser. You will feel these emotions to all topics within you.

Nobody is the Same

To become more in creative thinking

Is to identify nobody is the same

You cannot be the same

This is a divisive universe and you come to explore and clarify

To deliberately create what the individual wants and

In turn expand thought

Nothing is a Lesson

Nothing is a lesson

It is a becoming

It is adding to a greater broader experience of you

It becomes a greater knowing

No Doubt

All it takes is for you to believe

To focus on the desire, and

To have no doubt to the outcome

No Absence

Are you so in alignment that there is no absence of what you want to achieve?

Are you in an emotional state of bliss regardless of the things going on around you in the here and NOW

Most of all how much love and appreciation you have for you, if you have no appreciation of you, then how can you appreciate any improvement in conditions

Observation

Each experience you are having, you are creating, and each experience is realigning you to you.

Feel the emotion behind the experience

Observe you within these feelings

Don't place blame onto anyone else

These are your emotional responses to what you are asking for or observing

This applies to all aspects of life, whether in relationships, business, jobs, or a present condition

Origin of Thoughts

Think about your thoughts, how you start with a thought and then within minutes, that thought has deviated away from the first thought into thoughts of momentous proportions. Stop go back to the original thought if the flow of thought is a negative emotional thought, look at what created the thought, identify what and where these thoughts are taking you, how do you feel with the thought, do you want to go down this thought process, does it enhance you, or does it not serve you, and remember the thought is still a vibrational memory, it is to change the thought, and only think with new and better thoughts.

Observing

Everything is observational

It is in what you are observing

Is what you will bring in or become

Isn't it nice to be able to observe what you really want out of this real world, and through observing what you really do want you build your vibrational escrow of what you want, and then it is in the discovery into how to bring the vibrational escrow into realisation, so that you can live the dream. Everything is observational and it is in what you are observing is what you will bring in or become, it is choosing what you want to become and be, and if what you are observing is not what you want, it is to turn and look the other way.

Observing Conditions

Observing conditions keeps you in the receptive mode, of the condition

Observing conditions from other people's vibrations

Will become a condition

If you want it then keep on observing it

Power

All the power is here and now this is why it is the leading edge of thought, if you think past, present and future you are doing it right now, so whatever thought you are having is right now, if the human race realised that all thought is now, and how they want to translate thoughts to a vibration there is nothing more powerful than right now.

Powerful Interaction

Words cannot teach, it is your own guidance system within you that is the powerful interaction between you and you, once you get it then life will evolve into more desires, and more contrasting experiences and more clarity, and will forever keep on evolving.

Problem or Solution Oriented

If you are focusing on a problem

The problem stays

If you are asking for a solution or an improvement

Look only to the improvement or solution

Take your eyes and thoughts away from the problem

The more you observe the problem

the improvement or solution cannot come about

Pointing to Your Attraction

Thought processes of wanted and unwanted

Is pointing you to your attraction

You cannot think a thought without thinking the opposite of that thought

The thought of the wanted and unwanted

Is what is directing you to that thought

Pervasive Thought

A pervasive thought is

When you focus upon what you do like or do not like, you perpetuate that thought and that thought will become the dominate thought and this thought will be delivered to you.

All consciousness is thought, it is a pulsating energy of thought vibration every thought exists and these thoughts can be re-activated at any time, it is up to the individuals whether they want to re-activate a thought or to keep a thought active, it is in these thoughts that create a thought which creates a momentum of the thought which creates an emotion which is felt, it is for the individual to realise and clarify which thoughts they want to gather momentum to. It is to change the thoughts to what you really do want only.

IE; If you were to look for a better relationship, and consistently says I don't want to meet an abuser, you will meet an abuser, because that is your dominate thought pattern. You have to change your dominate thought pattern.

Pervasive Belief

Pervasive thought beliefs create illnesses

It is as simple as an illness, the parents talk about someone in the family having, as the humans call an incurable illness, they call it hereditary, it is only hereditary because they keep the illness alive, it is the thought that creates the thought to the illness, if they were to change the thought and leave it in the delete pile, it is then deleted, but the physical humans cannot seem to do this, they hear someone else talk about the illness and then the old thought re-emerges again and becomes active in their thoughts again, this is what creates the illness, if they were to delete and give it no oxygen the illness would become non-existent and an irrelevant topic. It is the power of thought focus is the creation, and then the physical human forms are bomb blasted and driven with the illness by media, by charity marches, by funded projects, this just keeps on perpetuating the process, it takes a very powerful physical human to override this thought and belief process, and when they get it, they will be set free of this incurable illness. The generations of families keep on perpetuating what they had onto their children, they have nothing better to say but with what they had, and then the innocents of the children take on their thought belief, and become what they are instead of what they want to be.

Powerful Flow

This is a powerful flow of vibrating universal energy.

You are all extensions of this flow

Of which is flowing to you and through you

Not separate from it

You are it

When you put the washing machine on you don't ask how it works or where the switch is, or how the flow of water gets in, you just know, turn on the switch the water flows in and you come out clean, what you want to feel is like a washing machine, the switch is on all the time this is the energy, the flow of water is always flowing this is you, what stops the flow is the dirty laundry with what you are activating into the mix, let the water energy flow and you truly will come out clean and in no resistance to your desires, but if you keep adding dirty laundry, the flow becomes sluggish and the process takes longer, clean up the dirty laundry and the laundry will sparkle, the energy switch is always flowing, it is just what type of laundry you have put into the machine.

Perpetuation

Every creation is thought in every thought is the imagination of the thought

What holds the imagination back is the observation to reality and holding onto old thoughts

You are bringing the reality in of which is in your imagination of what you want, in other words reality does not exist, it is the thoughts that bring about the reality

Reality only exists if you keep on perpetuating it

Reality then becomes the wanted or unwanted desires

Regret

Regret is not looking back

You can't change what has happened

Your focus is now focusing forward

This is where all the power is

Repetition

It is a repetition of speaking

Repetitive words in writing

It is all in the repetitive thoughts

It is through repetition that some form of recognition will finally attune you into your Source your Inner Being

Re-read and re-read the connection will, and does happen

It is all up to you and you alone

Repetition and Focus

Repetition and focus of thoughts and words

Appears to be the same

But in a different format always

It is through the repetitive words that recognition occurs, repetition in all forms will attune you, maybe not now but it does happen when you are ready to hear, and when you have a strong calling to want to feel good. You will listen or pick up a book and read the same words, and then one day the penny will just drop and then you will understand more and become more, it is all in the timing, and in the attuning in, and in the desire to become more, and to feel good.

Relationships

Seeking a relationship, the first step is the relationship between you and you, work on you first, define who you are, find alignment with your vibration, find alignment with what you have, or are creating into your vibrational reality of what you are wanting, not of what they are wanting, but the very core of what you want and who you are, and who you want to become.

The preparation is to define who you are, and who you allow into your experience, every relationship experience is expanding who you are, and expanding to who you want to become, it is the appreciation of well-being, it is reaching for behaviours that are good for you, it is the preparation of your thoughts and feelings of who you want to vibrate with, it is having fun along the way, it is creating what the intellect of the person is, it is about the vibration of the person with their own Inner Being, it is co-creating with your alignment of fullness with someone who will share and enhance your alignment of fullness, it is creating and expanding the lover into feeling it into being. Feel every aspect of what you want out of a partner, feel this partner as if the partner were here, even though you can't touch it or see it, your job is to grow an expansion of feeling this person into vibration, and when the non-physical can feel the vibration of your meaningful desire, the universe will match you up to a likeminded vibrational person, it is about timing and the right timing. Remember what you want and in what direction you are pointing too, is what you shall receive, in the wanted and unwanted. No exceptions.

What takes you away from a desired partner is the not having a partner, and where is the partner, and why haven't I a partner, looking for someone instead of building momentum of the desired partner. Not allowing of the universe to bring the thought building partner into reality. Not being happy without a partner, for you have to be happy with The Self-first and foremost. Not to look for someone to make you happy, it is your job to allow it to happen, and to create the partner into existence.

Tough call but that is creating at its best, and then, only the best will be delivered.

Relationships which are discorded

Relationships which are discorded is the asking for an improved condition and for those in these relationship conditions see the contrast and will have strong asking for a solution, they will have a strong asking for improvement, and the more they ask for improvement and believe in a solution the solution will come, it is all into what is being asked, and how you feel in the asking.

Relationship Attraction

Relationships are the process to discover what you really want in a relationship, every relationship is the building platform which you discover what you want in a relationship which you place into your vibration of what you really desire for you, it is building into the imagination of what you really do want, you identify you really like this in that person, you really like that in that person, and you bring these about into a vibration and this is felt by collective conscious and we work on delivering the person you have created, but if you look at what you don't like in that person or this person you will build up the very person that you do not want.

When you focus upon what you do not like, you perpetuate that thought and that thought will become the dominate thought and this thought will be delivered to you, it is to change the thoughts to what you really do want only and we mean only.

If you were to look at that person who is looking for a better relationship, and consistently says I don't want to meet a heavy drinker, she will meet a heavy drinker, because that is her dominate thought pattern.

Resistance

It is only through the resistance of the thought

That does not create what you want

The resistance being the doubt the disbelief and

Not trusting in the universal laws

Resistance holds you back

Resistance is treating the ones that do know and have tapped into this unseen energy as being crazy, but they deep down want to know how, and have a strong feeling to want to know, but in their own resistance they hold back.

Resistance is treating God as a secret of unexplained unseen phenomenon with which man has created many images for the very thing that is already in existence in each and every one who has re-emerged into a physical human form, it is through the opinions and the perception of what this image is, which has distorted massive proportions of separating you from discovering you, and this is the secret you are all that of which man calls as God.

Range of Emotions

The feeling range of emotions

Is unsurmountable

There are many emotions, fear is an emotion, love is an emotion, powerfulness is an emotion, satisfaction is an emotion, confidence is an emotion, hatred is an emotion, frustration is an emotion, anger is an emotion, eagerness is an emotion, excitement is an emotion, the range of emotions is unsurmountable, if you take the emotion of love there are many forms of love, it is an unconditional love emotion, love is a friendship emotion, feeling in love is an emotion, how you feel loving your pets, how you love in an activity, how you feel in love, how you feel viewing your world with joyous love, the love emotion is vast and you will discover the feelings of what it feels to feel in each emotion, but also identifying how it feels to the emotion, all these feelings guide you, when you feel if something you should do and are not sure, you will feel an angst within you, and when you feel yes! I want to do this or you feel an excitement within you, you will feel the urge to just go and nothing will hold you back, and your guidance system will give you thoughts it then begins to flow like a current, and this current is guiding you, it is not to counteract to those thoughts, this is your inner guidance system giving the thoughts, but so many people discredit these thoughts.

Stimulator of Thought

Thought is not converting but believing in one self and to feel better

It is the stimulator of thought to broaden your own perspective, and this is the ultimate focal point

No one can deny the wanting to feel good and

Have a better time in this life time

Seeking Love

It is not the love we are seeking in another,

It is the love that we are seeking within ourselves

Solutions

I am solution oriented

When I see there is a problem

I don't look at the problem only at the solution

You cannot eradicate a problem

It is in the refocusing of thought into the arena of a solution

I feel and imagine a solution and allow the universe to bring about the solution or a solution. It is to remember to detach from what is and allow the universe to bring about the solution. The solution is already in vibration, ask and then allow being the receiver of the solution

Source Energy

You are Source energy

You are the Source of well-being becoming more

You are as man calls God

You are here becoming more, and here to expand **you.**

You are deliberately creating and

You are deliberately manifesting your creations

Supplication Meaning

Supplicate the word, which is a begging word, this word indicates yearning, to pray humbly, and earnestly, this is not the way the universe plays out on emotions of begging and yearning, this indicator is begging and yearning for something which is not coming about.

To supplicate is not through the yearning, it is HOW you supplicate, it is asking, but it is in HOW you ask for it, and why you want it, not begging for what you want but telling the universe WHY you want the very thing you are asking for, and it is not asking for the very thing you want because the universe already knows this, but it is asking by emotional words, HOW you would feel, How the feeling of MORE, and IN becoming MORE, it is taking thought to the very thing you have asked for, to what it would be like, it would be MORE freedom, it would be MORE mobility, it would be MORE choices, it would be MORE expansion; play on these words you will feel the shift within yourself. You are all here to become MORE, not less than MORE. This is what growth and expansion is, it is all for the expansion of your vibrational Source. The most profound feeling of all is being satisfied with what is and eager for more, this is not looking to conditions that are not satisfying in your experience, but to change the thoughts to more satisfying, and the more satisfying feeling emotion will become more.

Separation from who you are

A negative thought is always a separation from what the spirit is feeling to that thought, a negative thought is the indication that the spirit does not believe in that thought, and does not join you in that thought, if the human form takes the negative thought into more negativity it will just get bigger and will be felt, the feeling breaks out into illnesses and ailments and headaches, and then into depressed mode.

Negative emotion is the indicator you are going the wrong way.

Spirit verses Human

You may have heard many times you are here, living here the spirit life living in a human form, this is the most truest concept to understand, it is changing your thoughts of not looking at the tangible but feeling the intangible which is the only existence of you, nothing else exists around you, the only thing that exists is the vibration of your Inner Being and the Collective Consciousness of this stream of energy.

Success

Success is in the imagination

The story you tell in your thoughts

Success is in the imagination and the story you tell in your thoughts. You consciously think and feel it into being of what you want, it is the energy thought form of the embryo building and growing with each thought, and then feeling the embryo build and grow from a thought form into a feeling emotion then into the gestation, this is what All the eyes and The Source feels and works toward.

The Spiritual Self

The spiritual Self requires a physical human form

For expansion of the spiritual Self

The physical form is the house for this expansion

The God force resides within

You and Me, as

You and Me

This God force is your Inner Being which is the older wiser part of you who has lived many life times, and now you are here as an extension of this older wiser part of you expanding your own energy stream for more expansion, to become more, and when you decide to depart the real world, your energy stream will become another physical being for the extension of your older wiser part of you, and this life stream will expand and become more, this creation is never ending.

Timing and Alignment

Timing and alignment are the same

The timing is allowing the gap

Of time to be drawn closer in time

This gap can be fulfilled in a day or in time

It is in trimming your time line

It is what you are outputting for the universe to feel and how magnified your vibration is

Imagine you are fishing with a lure that is your desire and the fish is the vibrating time and is us, you throw the line out, the lure is your thought desires sent out into the universe, you reel the line in a bit, we the time fish draws closer, the lure and fish being us feels this vibration, the line is reeled in again and the lure is feeling swimmingly fine, and we feel the alignment, the fish is getting closer, the fisherman the lure and the fish are now all in synchronicity, it is all drawing in nicely, and when everything is feeling positively delicious the fish will take the lure and the fisherman receives the manifestation. What slows the manifestation is the thought lure is projected, and then the fisherman thinks, is there any fish here, and then the lure snags with doubt, the lure gets wedged even further into the crack. It is to throw the thoughts and reel the fish and the lure together with no doubt. The excitement is to project out with the excitement of knowing, and glow with the excitement, and then to release the excitement, and just look at the water and the birds and bees and in appreciation of in the now, and when the projected thought arises again create the thought again and build into a more specific desire and then let it go and look at the birds and bees and find ways to appreciate what is in the now, do this process and the manifestation will come it is not a pipe dream it is a universal law if you are aligned in vibration it must come to you.

Thinking Mechanisms

Most everyone observes and has been directed to think what others think, when the discovery is realised that they are and we are thinking mechanisms, if we did not have thought, and future thoughts, desires, dreams and imagination we would stay dormant and unexpansive, if you consider thoughts where do these thoughts come from.

Thoughts

Thought is the life steam

You are here now on the leading edge of thought

The universe expands with your thoughts

The universe appreciates pure delicious new thoughts

With new thought brings in new expansion

We have expanded our thoughts to the here and now

Imagine the concept

Where new thought can lead the universe too, and

Lead your Source too

The Secret

The secret to the clarity is to do only what feels good

If it doesn't feel good

Then don't do it!

Thoughts that Inspire

Thoughts have the intent of the thought

Thoughts that inspire are the meaningful thoughts

Thoughts have the intent of the thought. Thoughts that inspire, are the meaningful thoughts, the meaningful emotional feeling thoughts, when thoughts are connected in true meaningful vibration and the laws of the universe can feel those meaningful intentions behind the thoughts and emotional feelings, the laws of the universe will bring through those wants and desires, when they know you are in complete stable vibration to that vibrational frequency.

Think Better Thoughts

True alignment with your Source begins with thoughts

Thoughts bring in emotional feelings

Think about your thoughts, how you start with a thought and then within minutes, that thought has deviated away from the first thought into thoughts of momentous proportions. Stop go back to the original thought if the flow of thought is a negative emotional thought, look at what created the thought, identify what and where these thoughts are taking you, how do you feel with the thought, do you want to go down this thought process, does it enhance you, or does it not serve you, and remember the thought is still a vibrational memory, it is to change the thought, and only think with new and better thoughts.

Think Feel and Focus

Think, feel and focus in the imagination of your wants

Think it, feel it, focus upon it

Reaching and savouring

Then reaching and savouring more

Think it and feel it even more

Build upon, and build upon, on the thoughts of the imagination

Feel how it feels, savour the feeling

Then think it more

The more you create the imagination the more it becomes

Until it is so tuned into your emotional essence

That it must come to you

Thought is the Life Stream

Thought is the life steam, you are here now on the leading edge of thought, and the universe expands with your thoughts.

The pure vibration looks at both aspects of the contrasting thought and the clarifying thought, and does not react to conditions, and understands the concept of each vibrating emotion; this is the freedom we all want to get to, and this is being in pure alignment. It is to identify the thought behind the thought, behind the thought, and behind the thought, you may have a thought but feel a mixed emotion to the thought behind the thought, and you will begin to feel the thoughts.

Thought is the life steam, you are here now on the leading edge of thought, the universe expands with your thoughts, the universe appreciates pure delicious new thoughts, with new thought brings in new expansion, we have expanded our thoughts to the here and now, imagine the concept where new thought can lead the universe too, and lead your Source too.

Think and Feel

Think and feel

Until you feel and think

This is allowing the thinking to come through after the feeling

This is being truly aligned with your Inner Being

Your higher Self

Speak only as long it is good

Think only as long as it is fun

Try as long as it is easy

See goodness in everyone

Make the best of what is and what is

Will improve and morph into a better feeling

This creates more improvement

This creates more expansion

Transmitter and Transponder

Everyone has or is questioning what the purpose of life is

What is it all about

It begins from conception

The understanding of emotional energy

This energy is a vibration

Emotion is bandied around and not even recognized as a form of communication between the two parts of a person

It is refocusing the mindset, and how the mind creates and

That the mind is the transmitter, and the transponder

The Law of Attraction

The Law of Attraction says

Nothing comes without giving your attention to it

And nothing stays without giving your attention to it

Watching you

You are being watched

Sounds kind of nutty, spooky or off the planet that these non-seen entities are watching us, it is collective consciousness of energy feeling the vibration of what we are emitting. They feel the vibration and they expand with our thoughts; thought is energy they love the deliciousness of a new thought, they love to see the formulation coming together in our thoughts, and they take immense joy when we are riding the wave of positive momentum. They feel the desirability and joy of seeing through our viewing eyes and The Source feels the pleasure we feel. When we expand, they expand, when we are truly in alignment of feeling really, really good, the universal forces will move vast energies in our direction so we may fulfil our desires.

Worthiness

You cannot control your surroundings or what is in the world

But you can control your vibration

Your feelings and emotions to feel good

To feel your worthiness

To feel your thoughts

Your own alignment between you and you

What is it is

Most people are looking at what is

The what is, is old thoughts

These old thoughts have a profound way of building more of the same

What is, is old news, it has already manifested

You are here to create new thoughts, new news

What Vibration are you on

True alignment with your Source begins with thoughts, thoughts bring in emotional feelings, and these are the indicators to what you are feeling at any point in time. How do you feel when these thoughts are positive or negative, how does the body feel, how does the emotions feel, are you introducing a heavy dark energy feeling or a light feeling, these are the indicators how aligned you are with your Inner Being. All of these energies are vibration, what vibration are you courting.

Worry

Worrying is using your imagination

To create something

You don't want

Wanted or Unwanted

Thought processes of wanted and unwanted

Is pointing you to your attraction

You cannot think a thought

Without thinking the opposite of that thought

The thought of the wanted and unwanted

Is what is directing you to that thought

What's Bothering You

Resistance to a thought

Ask what's bothering you, then realise it

Work through it

Release it and let it go

If you can't let it go

Look to another thought

You will feel the resistance of the bothering thought releasing

You are God

Religion talks about the devil and demons

The only demons and devils, is in what thoughts each individual is thinking

Are you playing out the demon or the godly part of you?

It is the perceived notion that god is separate from you, which has been instilled and projected by religion, peers, parents and teachers which has created disunity and a separateness from you and you. It is the lacking in the understanding with what is the purpose of life, and this attachment to belonging to something outside of you.

It has been the teachings and instilling of thoughts and emotions which has been un-recognized, or even considered as the form of gaining knowledge, through the feelings into one's own Inner-Being your Higher Self. It is the most talked about and the most controversial and dis-believed topic.

You Are Source Energy

You are Source energy becoming more

You are as man calls God

You are here becoming more and here to expand you

You are deliberately creating and deliberately manifesting your creations

I was asked why I use the word 'Source'

From a very young age I knew deep inside of me that I was and am, what is called God, but the God word never felt right to me, it implies religion, it made me feel very uncomfortable, I used to call it the <u>Great of divine</u> a changed version of God, it wasn't until I heard the word Source and Source energy I immediately tuned into me, no question it was instant. I prefer to use the term Source, or Inner Being. Source separates you from the prevalent teachings of what God is, there is only one God and that is you in all its pureness, to say that you are God is blaspheme in the eyes of religious teachings, and becomes the separateness of who you really are. This is the momentum process of the religious system which has created disunity, confusion and separateness within these teachings of who and what God is.

'I consecrate myself to meet their <u>need for growth in truth and Holiness</u>, I am not praying for these alone but also for the <u>future believers</u>' John 17: 19-21TLB

'Is it not written in the scriptures <u>ye are all Gods</u>' Psalm 82.6

'Love the lord <u>your</u> God with all <u>your</u> heart and all <u>your</u> soul and with all <u>your</u> mind and with all <u>your</u> strength' Mark 12:30.

The word <u>your</u> is taken out of context and distorted of the use of the word <u>your</u> which is a word used to indicate that <u>one belonging to oneself</u>. The kingdom of heaven is within; or (in your midst) Just taking a simple word and exaggerating it into a great almighty apart from you has taken <u>you</u> apart from <u>you</u>, You have separated yourself from who you really are, and that is you are God, not separate from it, but an extension of this stream of energy.

When creating you feel inferior in your creating, because after all that what you call God creates worlds, it is Y<u>ou</u> who Y<u>ou</u> are, as what man calls God here by virtue expanding and creating this world with your vibration and your thoughts, you have come here to be meaningful to this world and to fulfil the reason of being, and being the whole of who you are to the greater expansion of you and with your Inner Being, you are an extension of this collective conscious energy vibrational stream, you flow it, you are intertwined in this energy stream, and you are The Source (God), you are this life stream, and only you can dictate with you.

To really know God is to know how you feel, it is to know how you speak, it is to know how you think, it is know how you live, it is to know how to have fun, it is to know how to live joyfully, it is to know how to live happily, it is to know how you act, when you understand this simple logical interaction of communication between you and you, this is speaking to God, and when this understanding happens, and you begin being the receiver and feeling this energy, and then watch the results, you will create an expansion so powerful within.

'The kingdom of heaven is within' Luke 17-21

You are the Attractor

You are the attractor of your experience

You are the creator of your experience

You are here to create your creation

Most of all you came here as a willing and eager participant of The Source representing The Source, creating new expansion of thought, and eager to remember that you are The Source (God) you are pulsating vibrating energy in a human form and you have complete Oneness to all of this. You just have to tune yourself into this stream of energy and when you recognise, and are the receiver off receiving and acknowledging the impulses you just can't hold back what you do know, it is pure excitement energy, it is your given right to this energy, go with this flow of energy.

You are Not Separate

This life stream feels

Through this feeling gathers momentum of thought

Expands into emotions

This is what is felt

This is what creates

This is what you are to achieve

In this life time of living in the reality

Most importantly is to remember that you are

The Source you are not separate from it

The Author

The complexity of the mind, this thought mind is powerful, and it is not only felt by you, but also by your Higher Self, it is the Higher Self your Inner Being of which is your direct route, and only way to move forward to what you are asking for, and the way to make the discovery of what you are creating in thought to grow and grow and become a reality.

I discovered this powerful alignment, and I discovered how powerful one's thoughts are, and how you can feel the emotion within.

It is my powerful intention to write and speak of this awareness which everyone has.

I want to teach something that is the basis of which is what everyone needs to know.

YOU ARE GOD; EACH AND EVERY PERSON IS A GOD.

YOU ARE ETERNAL, AND WILL RISE AGAIN AND AGAIN.

YOU COME TO LIVE IN EACH LIFE TIME TO EXPAND YOUR ENERGY VIBRATION.

WHAT YOU HAVE BEEN TAUGHT FOR CENTURIES IS COMPLETELY MISGUIDED.

IT IS TIME TO RE-FOCUS AND RE-EXPAND YOUR THOUGHTS.

Now wouldn't it be nice to discover this powerful alignment which is within your eternal being, this eternal being is of well-being –it is alignment –it is happy –it is giving you the feeling indicators to your thoughts – it is of pure love – it is expanding with those positive thoughts – it does not flow with the negative thoughts which is why you feel such negative thoughts, it is your indicator telling you, that you are going the wrong way with those thoughts.

This is powerful guidance and it can be felt, all you have to do is feel how you feel in the thoughts and once you do, you will be the realiser and the expander into new manifestations, and boundless expansion of becoming more, and the way to all of this expansion is to live and feel happy no matter what is going on around you, if you do not like what is going on around you, it is to focus your thoughts to topics that feel really good to you and to feel this happy feeling place, it is for you to find the magic within, and then the magic will become.

The inspiring quotes were created within and reformatted from the books of Clarity, Thoughts Create, and Conversations with Consciousness.

More Inspiring Books by the Author

'Clarity'

978-0-6483420-0-7 eBook

978-0-6483420-4-5 paperback

Clarity is lining up with something that is really clear and I like it, it makes me feel good.

Clarity is in the transformation of the contrast into better feeling thoughts, not to avoid the negative thoughts but to transform and emphasis new better thoughts which makes me feel good.

The Law of Attraction says; nothing comes without your attention to it, and nothing stays without your attention to it.

You are bringing the reality in, of which is in your imagination of what you want, in other words reality does not exist, it is the thoughts that bring about the reality. Reality only exists if you keep on perpetuating it. Reality then becomes the wanted or unwanted desires

The true sign of intelligence is not knowledge but imagination: Albert Einstein

A belief is only a thought you keep thinking, if it feels good than you are in alignment with your Inner Being, if you feel angst or not feeling good, it is you separating you from your Inner Being, your Inner Being is not following you on this belief thought.

Simply co-creating at its best - all the abundance - all the wants - all the dreams - all the desires, are amassing in your vibrational escrow. It is simply the laws of the universe that make the desires become into beingness.

'Conversations with Consciousness'

978-0-6483675-6-7 paperback

978-0-6483675-7-4 eBook

Vibrational frequency energy is the transference of energy from one object to another or converted into form, very much disbelieved unless they can see it or touch.

If conceivable and all the humans which populate this earth, were to realise they are all transmitting mechanisms, and have this powerful signal which is never detached from them and is holding every desire you wish to become a reality, wouldn't you really like to tap into this resourceful guidance system.

Wouldn't it be nicer to live in your desires – drive your desires – work in your desires – play in your desires – have the best relationships;

Welcome! You have just made the best decision to broaden your perspective and the continuing motion forward in the stimulation of thought.

'Thoughts Create'

978-0-6483675-5-0 paperback

978-0-6483675-4-3 eBook

This is who you really are;

You are a vortex of energy residing in a physical house to expand your consciousness which is eternal.

You were eager to play the dance and to remember your vortex of energy.

This vortex of energy knows what you desire and when you want to leave this physical house and how.

You knew you could tap into this stream of energy and create with your thoughts and emotions to communicate with your vortex, you knew you could imagine whatever you wanted to be and do, and you knew you could trust the process and your vortex of energy will orchestrate the event.

You are the beholder of your thoughts.

Look at your thoughts, and you will discover everything that you are living is created by you, and not by anyone else.

These powerful thoughts are created by you, and to every thought there is an opposite, and with every thought is followed by an emotion.

Makes you kind of want to think about what you are thinking about.

'Back to Basics'

978-0-6483420-6-9 eBook

978-0-6483420-3-8 hardcover

978-0-6483675-0-5 paperback

This book focuses on inspiring the reader to examine alternatives to expensive chemical- based products. Discover how our common weeds are power-packed full of nutritional and medicinal healing. Learn to match the herb with the dish: which herbs to use in cooking. Learn how to make medicinal tinctures, poultice and herbal infusions. Have fun making natural alternatives for health, beauty and body products. Learn how to make mascarpone, sour cream, and ricotta. Have fun with these home recipes; you'll discover a new way to wellbeing.

'Back to Basics Harvest'

978-0-6483420-9-0 eBook

978-0-6483420-8-3 hardcover

978-0-6483675-1-2 paperback

161 recipes for creating chutneys, jams, vinaigrettes, sauces and jellies, just the way your grandmother used to, in the days when all good food was created in the home kitchen.

Suzanne Massee is passionate about home-grown and home-produced foods; her home-produced preserves have been sold throughout New Zealand.

Suzanne's restaurant was winner of the 2003 Wine and Food Challenge Award for Nelson-Marlborough – West Coast Region.

'Easy to Follow Baking Recipes'

978-0-6483675-2-9 eBook

This book is the outcome of years spent accumulating recipes, in a format that makes it easier to make the most of each season's harvests.

With easy to follow step by step recipes you can create delightful;

Baked Slices - Cakes - Biscuits - Christmas Cakes - Desserts - and Gluten Free recipes.

Added extra; how to make Dairy Products, did you know Mascarpone is so simple to make and yet so expensive to buy.

I had a cafeteria where I created the most delicious slices, the compliment of these slice recipes was through my father in-law who was the general manager and baker for a very popular bakery in Timaru in the South Island of New Zealand. These slice recipes have been handed down, and I have reduced the ingredient measurements from very large baker's trays to the household trays.

Social media

https://www.suzannemassee.com

https://www.amazon.com/-/e/B00DFBFRJK

https://www.smashwords.com/profile/view/suzannemassee

https://suzannemassee782038939.wordpress.com/blog/

https://www.facebook.com/massee19/

https://www.facebook.com/suzannem19/

https://www.instagram.com/suzanne.massee/

www.ingramcontent.com/pod-product-compliance
Lightning Source LLC
Chambersburg PA
CBHW031418290426
44110CB00011B/437